"Rich parents, smart parents"

"Exploring the Intersection of Rich and
Smart Parents"

By

William K. Lozano

Table of contents

Introduction

"Rich parents, smart parents" is a phrase that explores the different dimensions of parenting and how they can influence a child's development and future prospects. It highlights the interplay between financial resources and intellectual abilities within the context of parenting.

On one hand, rich parents typically have access to greater financial means, which can provide their children with a wide range of advantages. They can afford quality education, extracurricular activities, and resources that enhance their child's learning and personal growth. Financial stability can create an environment conducive to exploration, opportunities, and experiences that foster development.

On the other hand, smart parents refer to those who possess intellectual abilities, knowledge, and skills that can positively impact their child's upbringing. They prioritize education, critical thinking, and intellectual stimulation, providing their children with an environment rich in learning opportunities. These parents may emphasize the value of knowledge, curiosity, and personal growth, fostering an intellectual atmosphere within the family.

However, it is important to recognize that being rich or smart does not guarantee effective parenting or a successful outcome for a child. Parenting is a complex endeavor that involves a multitude of factors beyond financial resources and intelligence. Emotional support, nurturing, and instilling important values and character traits are just as crucial for a child's development.

Ultimately, the ideal scenario lies in a combination of both richness and intelligence in parenting, where financial stability is coupled with intellectual stimulation and emotional support. This dynamic can provide a strong foundation for a child's growth and prepare them for a well-rounded and successful future.

Chapter 1

Nurturing Emotional Intelligence in Children

Emotional intelligence (EI) refers to the ability to recognize, understand, and manage emotions, both in oneself and in others. It involves a set of skills and competencies that enable individuals to navigate their own emotions effectively, understand the emotions of others, and use that understanding to build healthy relationships and make informed decisions.

Emotional intelligence encompasses several key components:

Self-awareness: This involves recognizing and understanding one's own emotions, including strengths, weaknesses, values, and motivations.

Self-regulation: It involves managing and controlling one's emotions, impulses, and reactions in order to respond appropriately in different situations. This includes being able to adapt to change, stay calm under pressure, and handle stress effectively.

Motivation: This refers to the ability to harness emotions to drive and sustain motivation, set goals, and work towards them with a sense of enthusiasm and resilience.

Empathy: Empathy is the ability to understand and share the emotions of others. It involves being able to recognize and appreciate different perspectives, show compassion, and respond with sensitivity.

Social skills: Social skills encompass a range of abilities, such as effective communication, active listening, conflict resolution, collaboration, and leadership. These skills enable individuals to build and maintain positive relationships, influence others, and work well in teams.

Emotional intelligence is considered crucial in personal and professional success, as it affects various aspects of life, including decision-making, communication, conflict resolution, and overall well-being. It can be developed and improved through self-reflection, practice, and learning from experiences.

How to developed emotional intelligence in Children

Developing emotional intelligence in children is a crucial aspect of their overall growth and well-being. Here are some strategies and tips to foster emotional intelligence in children:

Model and express emotions: Children learn by observing others, so it's essential to model healthy emotional expression. Show them how to identify and regulate emotions by sharing your feelings in appropriate ways.

Teach emotional vocabulary: Help children build a rich emotional vocabulary by introducing and discussing a wide range of emotions. Encourage them to express how they feel in words, so they can better understand and communicate their emotions.

Validate their emotions: Show empathy and validate your child's emotions. Let them know that all emotions are acceptable and normal, even if their behavior may need to be addressed separately. Help them understand that it's okay to feel different emotions and that they can express them in healthy ways.

Teach emotional regulation: Guide children in developing strategies to manage their emotions. Encourage deep breathing, counting to ten, taking a break, or engaging in calming activities like drawing or listening to music when they feel overwhelmed.

Help them understand that they have control over their emotions and can choose how to respond.

Encourage perspective-taking: Foster empathy by encouraging children to consider other people's perspectives and emotions. Help them understand that everyone experiences different emotions and that their actions can impact others' feelings. This can promote kindness, understanding, and better relationships with others.

Problem-solving skills: Teach children problem-solving skills to help them manage challenging situations. Encourage them to think through problems, consider different solutions, and evaluate the potential outcomes. This will help them develop resilience and adaptability in dealing with emotional challenges.

Provide a safe and supportive environment: Create an environment where children feel safe expressing their emotions without fear of judgment or punishment. Encourage open communication, active listening, and mutual respect. Help them understand that mistakes and failures are opportunities for growth.

Foster emotional literacy through literature: Read books with emotional themes and characters to enhance children's understanding of emotions. Discuss the characters' feelings and encourage children to relate them to their own experiences. This can help develop emotional intelligence and empathy.

Practice mindfulness and self-awareness: Teach children to pay attention to their emotions, thoughts, and bodily sensations through mindfulness exercises. This cultivates self-awareness and helps children better understand their emotional states, leading to improved self-regulation.

Encourage social interactions: Provide opportunities for children to interact with peers, siblings, and adults to develop their social skills. Cooperative play, group activities, and collaborative projects can foster emotional intelligence by promoting empathy, sharing, and understanding others' perspectives.

Strategies for emotional intelligence parents
Emotionally Intelligent Parenting involves understanding and responding to your child's emotions in a supportive and empathetic manner. Here are some strategies for practicing emotionally intelligent parenting:

Recognize and validate emotions: Pay attention to your child's emotions and validate their feelings. Let them know that it's okay to feel a certain way and that you understand their emotions.

Teach emotional literacy: Help your child develop a vocabulary for their emotions. Teach them the names of different emotions and encourage them to express how they feel.

Model emotional regulation: Children learn by observing their parents' behavior. Show them healthy ways to manage and regulate emotions by modeling self-control, stress management, and problem-solving skills.

Foster open communication: Create a safe and non-judgmental space for your child to express their emotions and thoughts. Encourage them to share their feelings with you and listen attentively when they do.

Empathize and show understanding: Put yourself in your child's shoes and try to understand their perspective. Show empathy by acknowledging their emotions and providing comfort and support.

Set clear boundaries and expectations: Establish consistent and age-appropriate rules and boundaries for your child. Clear expectations can help them feel secure and understand what is acceptable behavior.

Use positive discipline strategies: Instead of harsh punishments or criticism, focus on teaching your child about consequences and problem-solving. Encourage them to take responsibility for their actions and guide them towards making better choices.

Encourage problem-solving skills: Help your child develop problem-solving skills by involving them in discussions about possible solutions to conflicts or challenges. Teach them to think through the consequences of their actions.

Foster resilience: Help your child develop resilience by teaching them to cope with setbacks and adversity. Encourage a growth mindset, emphasizing that mistakes are opportunities for learning and growth.

Practice self-care: Take care of your own emotional well-being so that you can be emotionally available for your child. Make time for self-care activities and seek support when needed.

Remember that every child is unique, and it's important to adapt these strategies to meet their individual needs. Emotional intelligence is a lifelong skill, and by practicing these strategies, you can help your child develop emotional awareness and resilience.

Chapter 2

Fostering a Growth Mindset

Understanding a fixed and a growth mindset

A fixed mindset refers to a psychological belief or attitude in which individuals believe that their personal qualities, such as intelligence or abilities, are fixed and cannot be significantly changed or developed over time. People with a fixed mindset tend to believe that their skills, talents, and intelligence are innate and static traits that determine their potential for success. They often avoid challenges, fear failure, and believe that effort is fruitless since they believe they have limited capacity to improve.

In a fixed mindset, individuals tend to view setbacks and failures as indications of their inherent limitations rather than opportunities for growth and learning. They may avoid taking risks or trying new things because they fear that their performance will reflect their fixed abilities and be judged negatively. As a result, they may shy away from challenges or give up easily when faced with obstacles.

This mindset can have significant implications for personal and professional development. People with a fixed mindset may not reach their full potential because they are reluctant to put in the effort needed for growth and improvement. They may also have a tendency to compare themselves to others and feel threatened by the success of others, as they perceive it as a reflection of their own limitations.

On the other hand, a growth mindset is the opposite of a fixed mindset. It is a belief that skills and abilities can be developed through dedication, effort, and learning. Individuals with a growth mindset embrace challenges, persist in the face of setbacks, and see failure as an opportunity for learning and improvement. They understand that their abilities are not fixed and can be enhanced with continuous effort and practice.

Developing a growth mindset can lead to greater resilience, motivation, and a willingness to take on challenges. It can also foster a love of learning, as individuals with a growth mindset are more likely to seek out new knowledge and skills. Cultivating a growth mindset involves recognizing and challenging fixed mindset thoughts and beliefs, reframing failures as learning opportunities, and focusing on the process of learning rather than just the outcome.

It's important to note that mindset is not fixed permanently, and individuals can shift from a fixed mindset to a growth mindset with awareness, effort, and practice.

How can fixed or Growth Mindset be generated

A fixed or growth mindset is a belief system that individuals have about their abilities and intelligence. While a fixed mindset assumes that these qualities are fixed and unchangeable, a growth mindset believes that they can be developed and improved through effort and learning. Here are some ways to generate or cultivate a growth mindset:

Awareness: Start by recognizing your own mindset and any fixed beliefs you may hold. Understand that your abilities and intelligence are not fixed traits but can be developed.

Embrace challenges: See challenges as opportunities for growth rather than as obstacles. Embrace them as chances to learn, develop new skills, and improve yourself.

Persistence and effort: Understand that effort is essential for growth and improvement. Embrace hard work and perseverance, even when faced with setbacks or failures. See them as learning opportunities rather than as indications of your abilities.

Emphasize the learning process: Focus on the process of learning rather than solely on the end result. Celebrate your efforts, progress, and the strategies you use to overcome obstacles. Acknowledge that mistakes and failures are part of the learning journey.

Cultivate a positive mindset: Develop a positive and optimistic outlook. Emphasize self-belief and avoid negative self-talk. Replace phrases like "I can't" with "I can't yet" to acknowledge that growth takes time and effort.

Seek feedback: Be open to receiving feedback from others and view it as an opportunity to learn and improve. Use feedback to identify areas of growth and set goals for further development.

Embrace learning opportunities: Take advantage of new experiences, challenges, and opportunities to expand your knowledge and skills. Step out of your comfort zone and be willing to try new things.

Surround yourself with growth-minded individuals: Engage with people who have a growth mindset. Their positive attitudes and perspectives can inspire and reinforce your own growth mindset.

Continuous learning and improvement: Develop a habit of lifelong learning. Engage in activities that stimulate your intellect, such as reading, attending workshops, or taking courses.

Celebrate progress: Recognize and celebrate your growth and achievements along the way. This will help reinforce your belief in your ability to develop and improve.

Remember, developing a growth mindset is a continuous process that requires consistent effort and self-reflection. Over time, these practices can help you shift from a fixed mindset to a growth mindset, enabling you to embrace challenges, learn from setbacks, and achieve greater personal and professional growth.

Growth Mindset for riches
A growth mindset can certainly contribute to parents' ability to achieve financial success, although it's important to note that financial success is not solely determined by mindset alone. Here are a few ways in which a growth mindset can

be beneficial for parents seeking to improve their financial situation:

Embracing learning and improvement: A growth mindset encourages individuals to see challenges and setbacks as opportunities for growth and learning. This mindset can help parents approach their financial situation with a positive outlook, seeking ways to improve their knowledge and skills related to personal finance, investing, entrepreneurship, and other areas that can lead to wealth accumulation.

Resilience in the face of obstacles: Financial success often involves taking risks, facing setbacks, and overcoming obstacles along the way. A growth mindset fosters resilience, allowing parents to bounce back from failures and setbacks, learn from their mistakes, and persist in their pursuit of financial goals.

Emphasizing effort and hard work: Parents with a growth mindset understand the importance of effort and hard work in achieving success. They instill these values in their children, teaching them the importance of perseverance, discipline, and a strong work ethic. By modeling these behaviors themselves, parents can create an environment that supports their own financial growth and potentially inspire their children to adopt a similar mindset.

Embracing opportunities for personal and professional development: A growth mindset encourages individuals to seek out opportunities for personal and professional growth. This could involve investing in education, acquiring new skills, networking, or pursuing entrepreneurial ventures. By continually developing themselves, parents can increase their earning potential and open up new avenues for wealth creation.

Building a positive mindset around money: Many people have limiting beliefs or negative attitudes towards money, which can hinder their financial progress. A growth mindset helps parents challenge these limiting beliefs and adopt a positive mindset around money. They become more open to opportunities, develop a healthy relationship with wealth, and are more likely to make sound financial decisions.

It's important to note that financial success is influenced by various factors, including economic conditions, access to resources, and personal circumstances. While a growth mindset can provide a valuable foundation for achieving riches, it should be complemented by strategic planning, financial literacy, and other practical skills related to money management.

Strategies for fostering growth mindset in children Cultivating a growth mindset in children is crucial for their personal development and long-term success. A growth mindset is the belief that intelligence, abilities, and talents can be developed through dedication, effort, and learning from mistakes. It empowers children to embrace challenges, persevere in the face of setbacks, and believe in their potential for growth.

Encourage a positive attitude towards challenges: Help children see challenges as opportunities for growth rather than obstacles to success. Teach them that with effort and determination, they can overcome difficulties and improve their skills.

Emphasize the process over outcomes: Shift the focus from grades and results to the learning process itself. Teach children to value hard work, effort, and the ability to learn from mistakes. Help them understand that progress is more important than immediate success.

Praise effort and perseverance: Instead of solely praising intelligence or talent, acknowledge and appreciate the effort children put into their work. Highlight their determination, resilience, and willingness to tackle difficult tasks. This encourages them to develop a strong work ethic.

Teach the power of "yet": Encourage children to add the word "yet" to their statements when faced with a challenge. For example, instead of saying, "I can't do this," they can say, "I can't do this yet." This small shift in language fosters a belief in their ability to grow and learn over time.

Provide constructive feedback: Offer specific and constructive feedback that focuses on the process and effort put forth rather than personal characteristics. Help children understand how they can improve and guide them towards effective learning strategies.

Model a growth mindset: Children often learn by observing their parents, teachers, and other influential figures. Demonstrate a growth mindset by embracing challenges, maintaining a positive attitude towards learning, and openly discussing your own mistakes and how you learned from them.

Encourage exploration and curiosity: Foster a sense of curiosity in children and encourage them to explore new interests and topics. Help them see learning as a lifelong journey rather than a destination.

By nurturing a growth mindset in children, we equip them with the essential skills of resilience, adaptability, and a love for learning. This mindset sets the foundation for their personal and academic growth, empowering them to reach their full potential in all areas of life.

Encouraging Resilience and Perseverance

Life is an unpredictable journey filled with countless obstacles and setbacks. Whether it's personal, professional, or academic, everyone faces challenges that test their limits. The ability to bounce back from adversity and continue striving for success is a quality known as resilience. Paired with perseverance, it forms a powerful combination that can propel individuals towards achieving their goals and dreams. In this article, we will explore the importance of encouraging resilience and perseverance and provide practical tips on how to develop and strengthen these essential qualities.

Understanding Resilience:

Resilience can be defined as the capacity to recover quickly from difficulties, adapt to change, and endure challenging circumstances. It is not about avoiding problems but rather about developing the mental and emotional fortitude to face them head-on. Resilient individuals possess a positive mindset, an unwavering belief in their abilities, and a determination to learn from their experiences.

Embracing failure as a stepping stone:
Resilience begins with accepting that failure is an inherent part of growth and success. Rather than viewing failure as a setback, encourage individuals to see it as an opportunity to learn, adapt, and improve. By reframing failure as a stepping stone to success, one can develop the resilience to keep moving forward despite temporary setbacks.

Cultivating a growth mindset:
A growth mindset fosters resilience by emphasizing the belief that abilities and intelligence can be developed through effort and dedication. Encourage individuals to adopt a growth mindset by focusing on their strengths, setting realistic goals, and embracing challenges as opportunities for

growth. This mindset shift empowers them to persist through difficulties, knowing that their abilities are not fixed but can be enhanced with time and effort.

Building a support network:
Human connections play a crucial role in fostering resilience. Encourage individuals to surround themselves with a supportive network of family, friends, mentors, and like-minded individuals who can provide emotional support, guidance, and encouragement during challenging times. Knowing that they have a reliable support system can significantly boost resilience and provide the motivation needed to persevere.

Understanding Perseverance:
Perseverance complements resilience by embodying the quality of steadfast persistence and unwavering determination. It is the ability to stay focused on long-term goals despite obstacles, setbacks, and

moments of self-doubt. Here are some strategies to encourage perseverance:

Clarifying goals and setting milestones:
Help individuals establish clear, meaningful goals and break them down into smaller, achievable milestones. By having a clear vision and a roadmap to success, individuals can maintain their focus and measure their progress along the way. Celebrating milestones also provides a sense of accomplishment, reinforcing the belief that perseverance leads to tangible results.

Developing self-discipline:
Perseverance often requires self-discipline to stay committed to the tasks at hand, especially when faced with distractions or competing priorities. Encourage individuals to cultivate self-discipline by creating daily routines, setting priorities, and practicing time management techniques. This helps

build the necessary habits and mental resilience to persevere when challenges arise.

Finding inspiration and motivation:
Inspiration and motivation play crucial roles in maintaining perseverance. Encourage individuals to seek out inspiring stories, role models, or mentors who have overcome similar challenges. Sharing stories of resilience and success can fuel motivation and remind individuals that they are not alone in their journey. Additionally, regularly reminding oneself of the reasons why they started on their path can reignite their passion and determination.

Resilience and perseverance are essential qualities that enable individuals to navigate life's challenges and achieve their goals. By fostering a growth mindset, building a support network, embracing failure as an opportunity for growth, clarifying goals, developing self-discipline, and finding inspiration, individuals can cultivate and strengthen their resilience and perseverance. Remember, setbacks are not permanent roadblocks but mere detours on the path to success. Encouraging these qualities will empower individuals to overcome obstacles, unlock their full potential, and ultimately lead a more fulfilling and successful life.

Educational Support and Enrichment

Education is the key to unlocking one's true potential and building a brighter future. However, the journey of learning can sometimes be challenging for students, requiring additional support and enrichment opportunities to maximize their growth. Educational support and enrichment programs play a vital role in nurturing students' abilities, enhancing their knowledge, and fostering a love for lifelong learning. In this article, we will explore the significance of educational support and enrichment in empowering minds and creating well-rounded individuals.

Addressing Individual Needs:

Every student is unique, with their own strengths, weaknesses, and learning styles. Educational support programs recognize and cater to these individual needs, providing tailored assistance to help students overcome academic hurdles. Whether it's through one-on-one tutoring, small-group interventions, or specialized resources, these programs offer targeted support to ensure students receive the attention they require. By addressing individual needs, educational support fosters a sense of inclusivity, boosts confidence, and enables students to reach their full potential.

Filling Learning Gaps:
In a fast-paced educational environment, students may occasionally experience learning gaps, missing out on essential concepts or skills. Educational support programs step in to bridge these gaps, providing additional instruction, reinforcement, and remedial support. By focusing on specific areas of weakness, students can catch up with their peers and develop a strong foundation for future learning. These programs ensure that no student is left behind and help them progress academically with increased confidence and understanding.

Enrichment Opportunities:

While educational support programs address academic challenges, enrichment programs go beyond the core curriculum, offering students opportunities to explore and expand their horizons. Enrichment activities encompass a wide range of subjects, including art, music, sports, STEM (science, technology, engineering, and mathematics), and leadership development. These programs encourage students to pursue their passions, cultivate new skills, and discover hidden talents. By exposing students to diverse experiences, enrichment programs foster creativity, critical thinking, and a well-rounded approach to education.

Holistic Development:

Educational support and enrichment programs contribute to the holistic development of students.

They not only focus on academic excellence but also foster social and emotional growth. These programs provide a nurturing environment where students can build relationships, develop teamwork skills, and enhance their self-esteem. By participating in extracurricular activities, students learn valuable life lessons such as discipline, time management, and resilience, which are crucial for success beyond the classroom. Educational support and enrichment programs create well-rounded individuals who are prepared to face the challenges of the real world.

Lifelong Learning:
One of the primary goals of education is to instill a love for lifelong learning. Educational support and enrichment programs play a pivotal role in nurturing this passion. By offering engaging and interactive learning experiences, these programs ignite curiosity and stimulate intellectual growth. They introduce students to new ideas, perspectives,

and opportunities for personal and intellectual exploration. By promoting a positive attitude towards learning, educational support and enrichment programs equip students with the tools they need to continue their educational journey long after their formal schooling.

Educational support and enrichment programs are essential pillars of a comprehensive education system. They provide personalized assistance, bridge learning gaps, offer enrichment opportunities, contribute to holistic development, and foster a love for lifelong learning. By investing in these programs, we empower minds, unlock individual potential, and create a brighter and more equitable future for all. Let us continue to prioritize and support educational support and enrichment initiatives, ensuring that every student has the opportunity to thrive and succeed.

Choosing the Right School for Your Child

Selecting the right school for your child is one of the most important decisions you'll make as a parent. It sets the foundation for their education, personal growth, and overall well-being. With a myriad of options available, finding the perfect fit can be overwhelming. However, by considering key factors and asking the right questions, you can navigate the selection process with confidence and ensure a positive educational experience for your child. This article provides a comprehensive guide to help you choose the right school for your little one.

Understand Your Child's Needs:

Every child is unique, with different personalities, learning styles, and interests. Begin by assessing your child's needs and preferences. Consider their academic strengths, extracurricular interests, social skills, and any special requirements they may have. Understanding your child's unique qualities will help you identify schools that cater to their individual needs.

Research School Options:
Thorough research is crucial to finding the right school. Start by gathering information about the schools in your area. Explore their websites, read reviews, and talk to other parents to get a sense of each school's reputation, educational philosophy, and values. Consider factors such as class sizes, teacher qualifications, curriculum, extracurricular activities, and facilities.

Visit Schools:
Visiting prospective schools is essential to get a firsthand experience of their environment and culture. Schedule appointments to tour the campuses, meet the staff, and observe classrooms. Pay attention to the atmosphere, the interactions between teachers and students, and the overall learning environment. This will help you gauge

whether the school aligns with your child's needs and educational goals.

Consider Location and Commute:
The proximity of the school to your home or workplace is an important practical consideration. Evaluate the commute time and logistics involved in getting your child to and from school. A long and exhausting commute can impact your child's well-being and overall performance. Additionally, consider the safety of the neighborhood surrounding the school.

Evaluate Academic Programs:
Examine the school's academic programs and curriculum. Does it offer a well-rounded education that fosters critical thinking, creativity, and problem-solving skills? Are there opportunities for enrichment programs, advanced courses, or extracurricular activities that align with your child's interests? Look for a school that strikes a balance

between academic rigor and a holistic approach to education.

Assess Student Support Services:
Different children may require varying levels of support. Consider the availability of support services such as special education programs, counseling, and resources for students with diverse learning needs. A school that offers a comprehensive range of support services ensures that your child's individual requirements are met, allowing them to thrive academically and emotionally.

Parent-Teacher Communication:
Strong parent-teacher communication is vital for your child's success. Inquire about how schools involve parents in their educational journey. Do they have regular parent-teacher meetings, open houses, or online portals to track your child's progress? A school that values collaboration and

keeps parents informed fosters a positive partnership between home and school.

Consider School Culture:
The school's culture plays a significant role in shaping your child's values and character development. Assess the overall atmosphere, values, and disciplinary policies of each school. Look for an inclusive and nurturing environment that promotes respect, empathy, and cultural diversity. Pay attention to how the school handles conflict resolution and promotes a positive student-teacher relationship.

Financial Considerations:
Consider the financial aspect of choosing a school. Evaluate tuition fees, additional costs for uniforms, textbooks, transportation, and extracurricular activities. While private schools may offer specialized programs, they come with a higher price tag. It's important to find a school that aligns with

your budget without compromising on quality education.

Trust Your Instincts:

Ultimately, trust your instincts and listen to your child's feedback. Involve your child in the decision-making process if they're old enough. A school that resonates with your values and beliefs, and that your child feels comfortable and excited about, is likely the right choice.

Choosing the right school for your child requires careful consideration of their unique needs, preferences, and the available options. By conducting thorough research, visiting schools, and evaluating factors such as academic programs, support services, and school culture, you can make an informed decision. Remember, finding the right school sets the stage for your child's educational journey, helping them unlock their full potential and shape a bright future.

Balancing Academic Pressure and Well-rounded Development

In today's fast-paced world, students face increasing academic pressure to excel in their studies. The pursuit of good grades and academic achievements has become the primary focus for many, often overshadowing other important aspects of a well-rounded development. However, it is crucial to find a balance between academic success and holistic growth, as fostering various skills and interests can lead to a more fulfilling and prosperous future. This article explores the importance of balancing academic pressure with well-rounded development and offers practical strategies to achieve this equilibrium.

The Downsides of Excessive Academic Pressure

While academic excellence is undoubtedly important, solely prioritizing academic achievements can have detrimental effects on students' overall well-being. Here are a few downsides of excessive academic pressure:

Diminished Mental Health: The constant race for higher grades and the fear of failure can lead to heightened stress, anxiety, and even depression among students. Mental health issues can negatively impact both academic performance and personal growth.

Limited Skill Development: Focusing solely on academics can restrict students' opportunities to explore and develop other essential skills such as creativity, critical thinking, problem-solving, communication, and leadership abilities. These skills are vital for success in the real world.

Lack of Emotional Intelligence: Emotionally intelligent individuals possess empathy, self-awareness, and strong interpersonal skills. Overemphasis on academics may result in neglecting the development of emotional intelligence, hindering students' ability to navigate social situations effectively.

Strategies for Balancing Academic Pressure and Well-rounded Development

Time Management: Efficient time management is key to balancing academic commitments and extracurricular activities. Prioritize tasks and create a schedule that allocates dedicated time for studies, hobbies, physical activity, and relaxation. This approach ensures a well-rounded approach to personal growth.

Pursue Passionate Interests: Encourage students to explore their passions and interests outside the classroom. Engaging in extracurricular activities such as sports, music, arts, or community service allows for the development of diverse skills, enhances self-confidence, and fosters a sense of fulfillment.

Encourage Critical Thinking and Creativity: Schools and parents should encourage independent thinking, problem-solving, and creativity. Engage students in discussions, debates, and open-ended projects that promote intellectual curiosity and allow for the application of knowledge in practical ways.

Foster a Supportive Environment: Create an environment that supports and celebrates well-rounded development. Schools, parents, and communities should recognize and appreciate achievements beyond academics, such as leadership roles, artistic accomplishments, or contributions to the community. This helps students understand that success extends beyond grades.

Stress Management Techniques: Teach students stress management techniques such as mindfulness, deep breathing exercises, regular physical activity, and sufficient sleep. These practices enhance resilience, reduce anxiety, and promote overall well-being.

Set Realistic Expectations: Parents and educators must set realistic expectations for academic performance, considering each student's unique abilities and interests. Encourage students to pursue their personal best rather than striving for perfection, fostering a healthier mindset and reducing undue pressure.

Striking a balance between academic pressure and well-rounded development is crucial for students' overall growth and success. By nurturing various skills and interests outside of the classroom, students can enhance their personal and professional prospects. It is vital for schools, parents, and communities to collectively create an environment that values and supports holistic development, appreciating achievements beyond academic performance. By implementing strategies such as effective time management, pursuing passions, fostering critical thinking and creativity, managing stress, and setting realistic expectations, students can lead fulfilling lives that encompass both academic success and well-rounded development.

Chapter 3

Financial Literacy and Responsibility

Financial literacy refers to the knowledge and understanding of financial concepts and skills that are necessary for individuals to make informed and effective decisions about their personal finances. It involves being able to comprehend and apply financial concepts such as budgeting, saving, investing, borrowing, and managing debt.

Financial responsibility, on the other hand, refers to the ability to manage one's finances in a prudent and accountable manner. It includes taking ownership of one's financial well-being, making sound financial decisions, and being accountable for the consequences of those decisions. Financial responsibility involves living within one's means, setting financial goals, and adopting responsible financial behaviors.

Both financial literacy and responsibility are crucial for individuals to achieve financial well-being and make informed choices about their money. Financial literacy provides the knowledge and skills necessary to understand and navigate the complex world of personal finance, while financial responsibility ensures that individuals apply that knowledge effectively and take ownership of their financial decisions and actions.

Teaching Children about Money
Teaching children about money is an essential life skill that can set them up for financial success in the future. Here are some strategies you can use to educate children about money:

Start early: Introduce the concept of money and its value to children at a young age. Even preschoolers can begin to understand basic money concepts like counting and recognizing different coins and bills.

Lead by example: Children learn a lot from observing their parents' behavior. Demonstrate responsible financial habits by budgeting, saving, and making wise spending decisions. Discussing your financial choices and explaining why you make certain decisions can be beneficial.

Use everyday situations: Look for opportunities to teach children about money in daily life. For example, involve them in grocery shopping and explain how you compare prices or make choices based on a budget. Teach them to differentiate between wants and needs.

Provide an allowance: Consider giving children a regular allowance to help them learn about money management. Encourage them to allocate a portion of their allowance for saving, spending, and giving. This helps them develop budgeting skills and learn the importance of saving for the future or helping others.

Set savings goals: Help your child set short-term and long-term savings goals. For younger children, these goals might be small, like saving for a toy or game. As they get older, encourage them to save for larger purchases or future expenses like college or a car.

Open a bank account: When your child is old enough, help them open a savings account. This will teach them about the banking system, interest, and the benefits of saving money in a secure place. Involve them in the process of depositing and tracking their savings.

Teach budgeting: Teach children the importance of budgeting by involving them in family budget discussions. Help them create their own budget for managing their money, whether it's from allowances, gifts, or part-time jobs. Encourage them to track their income and expenses to understand where their money is going.

Introduce entrepreneurship: Encourage children to explore entrepreneurial activities like starting a small business or doing odd jobs for neighbors or family members. This can teach them valuable lessons about earning money, managing finances, and taking responsibility.

Discuss financial topics: As children grow older, engage them in conversations about more complex financial topics like credit, loans, investments, and taxes. Explain these concepts in age-appropriate language, relating them to real-life scenarios whenever possible.

Be patient and reinforce learning: Money management skills take time to develop. Be patient with your child's progress and reinforce the lessons regularly. Encourage questions, provide guidance, and offer positive reinforcement when they demonstrate responsible financial behavior.

Instilling Good Financial Habits

Instilling good financial habits in children is crucial for their long-term financial well-being. Here are some tips on how to do so:

Start early: Introduce the concept of money and financial responsibility from a young age. Teach them the value of money and the importance of saving, spending wisely, and giving.

Lead by example: Children learn by observing their parents and caregivers. Display responsible financial behaviors such as budgeting, saving, and making informed purchase decisions. Avoid impulsive buying or excessive consumerism.

Teach budgeting: Help your children understand the concept of budgeting by giving them an allowance or helping them earn money through chores or small jobs. Encourage them to divide their money into different categories like savings, spending, and giving. This helps them prioritize and plan their expenses.

Set savings goals: Teach children the habit of saving by encouraging them to set goals for things they want to buy. This helps them understand the value of delayed gratification and the importance of saving for the future.

Explain the difference between needs and wants: Teach children to distinguish between essential needs and discretionary wants. Help them understand that it's important to prioritize needs over wants and make responsible spending choices.

Involve them in financial decisions: As appropriate for their age, involve children in discussions about financial decisions. This can include shopping for groceries, comparing prices, or discussing major purchases. It helps them understand the thought process behind financial choices.

Encourage entrepreneurship and work ethic: Support your children in exploring entrepreneurial ventures or encouraging them to take up part-time jobs or internships when they are old enough. This instills a sense of work ethic, money management, and financial independence.

Teach the value of giving: Encourage your children to develop a habit of giving to others in need or to charitable causes. This cultivates empathy and a sense of social responsibility.

Educate about credit and debt: As your children grow older, teach them about credit, borrowing, and the implications of debt. Help them understand the importance of responsible credit card use and the potential consequences of excessive debt.

Practice open communication: Create an environment where your children feel comfortable discussing financial matters openly. Encourage them to ask questions and seek guidance when needed.

The importance of instilling good financial habits in children cannot be overstated. It sets the foundation for their financial future, enabling them to make informed decisions, avoid debt, and work towards their goals. Good financial habits also promote a sense of responsibility, self-discipline, and financial security later in life.

Preparing children for financial independence
Teaching children about money management and financial independence is an essential life skill that will benefit them throughout their lives. By instilling good financial habits early on, parents can empower their children to make smart financial decisions, develop a strong work ethic, and achieve financial independence in the future. Here are some key strategies for preparing children for financial independence.

Start early: It's never too early to begin teaching children about money. Even at a young age, you can introduce basic concepts such as saving, spending, and giving. Use real-life examples and make it fun by using piggy banks or savings jars to help them visualize their money growing.

Teach the value of money: Help children understand the value of money by encouraging them to earn it. Assign age-appropriate chores and offer monetary rewards for completing them. This will teach them the connection between work and income, instilling a strong work ethic from an early age.

Set savings goals: Encourage children to set savings goals for things they want to buy. Whether it's a new toy or a bigger purchase like a bicycle, teach them the importance of saving up for what they want rather than relying on instant gratification. This will instill discipline and delayed gratification, essential skills for financial independence.

Introduce budgeting: Teach children the concept of budgeting by giving them a set amount of money each week or month and helping them allocate it for different purposes such as saving, spending, and giving. This will help them understand the importance of managing their money wisely and making informed choices.

Foster entrepreneurial skills: Encourage children to explore their entrepreneurial spirit by supporting their small business ideas or encouraging them to take on part-time jobs when they are old enough. This will teach them valuable lessons about financial responsibility, customer service, and the rewards of hard work.

Teach about debt and credit: As children grow older, it's important to educate them about the responsible use of debt and credit. Explain the consequences of excessive debt and the importance of paying bills on time. Introduce the concept of credit scores and the impact they can have on future financial opportunities.

Lead by example: Children learn best by observing their parents' behavior. Set a positive example by practicing sound financial habits yourself. Discuss your financial decisions with your children, such as saving for retirement or making a big purchase, to help them understand the reasoning behind your choices.

Emphasize the importance of education: Education is a crucial aspect of financial independence. Encourage your children to pursue higher education or vocational training to enhance their job prospects and earning potential. Help them understand the long-term benefits of investing in their education.

Teach them about investing: Introduce the concept of investing to children as they grow older. Teach them about stocks, bonds, and other investment vehicles. Encourage them to start investing early and emphasize the power of compound interest over time.

Encourage philanthropy: Instill a sense of social responsibility by teaching children the importance of giving back. Encourage them to donate a portion of their money or time to charitable causes. This will help them develop empathy, gratitude, and an understanding of the bigger picture beyond their own financial goals.

By following these strategies, parents can lay a strong foundation for their children's financial independence. Remember, it's not just about teaching children how to earn money but also about developing the skills to manage it wisely. With proper guidance and practical lessons, children can grow up to be financially responsible adults who are equipped to navigate the complexities of the financial world and achieve independence.

Chapter 4

Balancing Work and Family Life

Being a parent is a rewarding and fulfilling experience, but it also comes with a multitude of responsibilities. Juggling work and family life can be challenging, but with the right strategies and mindset, it is possible to achieve a healthy balance. Here are some key considerations and practical tips for parents striving to strike the right equilibrium between their careers and family time.

Prioritize and Set Realistic Expectations: Understanding your priorities is crucial in maintaining a healthy work-life balance. Take the time to identify what matters most to you and your family. It's essential to set realistic expectations for yourself and accept that you can't do everything perfectly. Establish clear boundaries between work and family time and communicate them to your employer, colleagues, and loved ones.

Effective Time Management: Efficient time management is vital for parents. Create a schedule that accounts for both work and family commitments. Use calendars, planners, or digital tools to organize your time effectively. Prioritize tasks, delegate responsibilities when possible, and learn to say no to non-essential activities. Make sure to include quality family time in your schedule and treat it as a non-negotiable commitment.

Communicate and Coordinate: Open and honest communication is key to maintaining a healthy work-life balance. Discuss your needs and concerns with your partner, family members, and employer. Work together to find solutions and compromises that accommodate everyone's needs. Coordinate schedules, share household responsibilities, and support each other in managing work and family commitments.

Flexible Work Arrangements: Explore flexible work arrangements that can help you better manage your time. Consider options like flextime, telecommuting, or part-time work if they align with your career and family goals. Discuss these possibilities with your employer and highlight how they can benefit both you and the company.

Embrace Self-Care: Taking care of yourself is crucial to maintaining a healthy work-life balance. Find time for activities that recharge and rejuvenate you, whether it's exercise, hobbies, or simply relaxation. Prioritizing self-care ensures you have the energy and emotional well-being to be present and engaged with your family.

Seek Support: Don't be afraid to ask for help when needed. Reach out to family, friends, or trusted caregivers who can provide support with childcare or other responsibilities. Consider joining parenting groups or seeking professional counseling if you feel overwhelmed. Remember, seeking support is a sign of strength, not weakness.

Be Present and Mindful: When you are with your family, strive to be fully present and engaged. Put away distractions like phones or work-related concerns and focus on quality time with your loved ones. Practice mindfulness techniques to help you stay present and appreciative of the precious moments you share.

Manage Guilt and Prioritize Quality Over Quantity: Many parents experience guilt when trying to balance work and family life. It's important to remember that quality time spent with your children matters more than the quantity of time. Be intentional in creating meaningful interactions and make the most of the time you have together.

Balancing work and family life is an ongoing process that requires regular evaluation and adjustments. Remember that achieving a perfect balance is not always realistic, but with mindful choices, effective communication, and self-care, parents can find a satisfying equilibrium that allows them to excel both in their careers and as nurturing parents.

Parents involvement and quality time
Parental involvement and quality time play a crucial role in a child's development and overall well-being. In today's fast-paced world, where both parents often have demanding jobs and numerous commitments, it can be challenging to find the balance between work and family life. However, making a conscious effort to prioritize parental involvement and quality time can have a profound impact on a child's life.

Parental involvement goes beyond simply being physically present in a child's life. It encompasses emotional support, active engagement, and consistent communication. When parents are actively involved, children tend to have better academic performance, improved social skills, and enhanced emotional regulation. They feel valued, secure, and develop a sense of belonging.

Quality time refers to the undivided attention parents give to their children, where distractions are minimized, and genuine connection is fostered. It is not about the quantity of time spent but the quality of the interactions. Engaging in activities together, such as reading, playing games, cooking, or simply having meaningful conversations, can create lasting memories and strengthen the parent-child bond.

Here are some key benefits of parental involvement and quality time:

Enhanced Communication: Spending quality time with children provides opportunities for open and honest communication. It allows parents to listen attentively to their children's thoughts, concerns, and dreams. Regular conversations build trust and promote a deeper understanding of each other.

Emotional Well-being: When children receive parental involvement and quality time, they feel loved, supported, and emotionally secure. This helps them develop a positive self-image, boosts their self-esteem, and equips them with the emotional tools needed to navigate life's challenges.

Academic Success: Parents who are actively involved in their child's education create a positive learning environment at home. They can support and reinforce what their children are learning in school, helping them to excel academically. Additionally, parental involvement shows children that education is important and encourages them to take their studies seriously.

Social Skills Development: Quality time spent with parents allows children to learn and practice essential social skills. Through engaging in conversations, playing games, and participating in activities together, children develop empathy, cooperation, and problem-solving abilities. They also learn how to interact with others and develop healthy relationships.

Character Building: Parental involvement and quality time provide opportunities for imparting values and teaching important life lessons. Parents can share their experiences, values, and moral beliefs, instilling in their children a strong sense of ethics and guiding them towards becoming responsible and compassionate individuals.

It is important to note that parental involvement and quality time should be consistent and age-appropriate. As children grow, their needs change, and parents must adapt their involvement accordingly. Flexibility and understanding are crucial to creating a nurturing environment where children feel heard, respected, and supported.
parental involvement and quality time are essential components of a child's upbringing. By actively participating in their child's life and dedicating quality time, parents can strengthen their relationship, promote emotional well-being, and contribute to their child's overall development. Remember, the moments we spend with our children today will shape their future and create lasting memories for both parent and child alike.

Coping with the Pressure of Success

Success is often seen as the pinnacle of achievement, something we strive for in our personal and professional lives. However, along with success comes a unique set of challenges and pressures that can be overwhelming if not properly managed. Coping with the pressure of success is essential for maintaining our well-being and ensuring continued growth. Here are some strategies to help navigate this often tricky terrain.

Set Realistic Expectations: When we achieve success, it's easy to fall into the trap of setting even higher expectations for ourselves. While it's important to aim high, it's equally crucial to set realistic goals. Unrealistic expectations can lead to constant pressure and dissatisfaction, making it difficult to appreciate and enjoy our accomplishments. Be mindful of what is achievable and give yourself permission to celebrate your successes, no matter how small.

Embrace Failure as a Learning Opportunity: The fear of failure can intensify when success is at stake. However, it's important to recognize that setbacks and failures are inevitable parts of any journey. Instead of letting failure discourage you, view it as a valuable learning opportunity. Analyze what went wrong, make adjustments, and use the experience to grow and improve. Remember, success is rarely a straight path, and resilience in the face of failure is key to long-term success.

Prioritize Self-Care: As the demands of success increase, it becomes crucial to prioritize self-care. Take time for activities that bring you joy and help you relax. Engage in regular exercise, practice mindfulness or meditation, and ensure you get enough sleep. Set boundaries to maintain a healthy work-life balance and avoid burnout. Taking care of yourself physically, mentally, and emotionally is essential for coping with the pressures that success brings.

Seek Support: It's easy to feel isolated when dealing with the pressures of success. Surrounding yourself with a strong support system can make a significant difference. Reach out to trusted friends, family members, or mentors who can offer guidance, encouragement, and a listening ear. Connect with like-minded individuals who have experienced similar challenges and learn from their insights. Remember, seeking support is not a sign of weakness but a wise decision that can help you navigate the complexities of success.

Maintain Perspective: Success can sometimes cloud our judgment and make us lose sight of what truly matters. It's essential to maintain perspective and keep your values and priorities in check. Remember that success is not just about achievements and accolades but also about personal growth, happiness, and meaningful relationships. Take time to reflect on your values, revisit your goals, and ensure that your definition of success aligns with your overall well-being and fulfillment.

Coping with the pressure of success is a lifelong journey. It requires self-awareness, resilience, and a willingness to adapt. By setting realistic expectations, embracing failure, prioritizing self-care, seeking support, and maintaining perspective, you can navigate the challenges that come with success while staying grounded and true to yourself. Remember, success is not just about the destination but also about the journey, and how you handle the pressure along the way shapes your overall experience of success.

Chapter 5

Cultivating Values and Ethics

Cultivating values and ethics is an important aspect of personal and societal development. Values are the principles or standards that guide our behavior and decision-making, while ethics refer to the moral principles that govern our actions and interactions with others. By consciously cultivating values and ethics, individuals and communities can foster a more harmonious and ethical environment. Here are some key points to consider when cultivating values and ethics:

Self-reflection: Begin by reflecting on your own values and ethics. Consider what matters most to you, what principles you want to uphold, and how you want to interact with others. This self-reflection helps you understand your own moral compass and lays the foundation for cultivating values and ethics.

Education and awareness: Continuous learning and staying informed about ethical principles, moral dilemmas, and different perspectives are crucial. Engage in activities that broaden your understanding of ethics and values. Read books, attend seminars, and engage in discussions to explore different ethical frameworks and approaches.

Lead by example: Cultivating values and ethics starts with your own behavior. Act in alignment with your values and be a role model for others. Show integrity, honesty, and respect in your interactions with others. Your actions speak louder than words, and by leading by example, you can inspire others to follow ethical paths.

Encourage open dialogue: Create an environment where open and respectful discussions about values and ethics are encouraged. Engage in conversations with family, friends, colleagues, and community members to explore ethical dilemmas and perspectives. This helps develop a deeper understanding and respect for different viewpoints.

Practice empathy and compassion: Cultivate empathy and compassion towards others. Consider the impact of your actions on others and strive to treat everyone with fairness and kindness. Empathy allows you to understand different perspectives and make ethical decisions that consider the well-being of others.

Foster a culture of integrity: Encourage honesty, transparency, and accountability in personal and professional settings. Promote ethical behavior by addressing unethical practices and supporting those who uphold ethical values. Foster a culture that values integrity and rewards ethical decision-making.

Continuous self-improvement: Cultivating values and ethics is an ongoing process. Continuously evaluate your actions and decisions to ensure they align with your values and ethical principles. Seek feedback from others, reflect on your choices, and be open to personal growth and development.

Contribute to the community: Extend your ethical principles beyond personal interactions and contribute to the betterment of your community and society. Engage in volunteer work, support causes that align with your values, and advocate for ethical practices in various aspects of life. cultivating values and ethics is a personal journey that requires ongoing effort and self-reflection. By consciously integrating ethical principles into your life, you can contribute to a more ethical and values-driven world.

Instilling Moral Values in Children

Instilling moral values in children is an important aspect of their overall development. Here are some strategies and approaches that can help in this process:

Be a role model: Children learn by observing and imitating their parents and caregivers. It's crucial to model the behavior and values you want to instill in your child. Be mindful of your actions and strive to demonstrate honesty, respect, kindness, empathy, and other positive values in your daily life.

Communicate and discuss: Engage your child in open and age-appropriate discussions about moral values. Talk about why certain actions are right or wrong, and encourage them to share their thoughts and perspectives. Discuss real-life examples and ethical dilemmas to help them understand the importance of making morally sound decisions.

Set clear expectations: Establish clear expectations for behavior and reinforce positive actions. Consistently praise and reward your child when they demonstrate values such as honesty, fairness, and compassion. Similarly, address and correct inappropriate behavior, explaining the reasons behind your concerns.

Teach empathy and compassion: Help your child develop empathy by encouraging them to understand and consider other people's feelings and perspectives. Teach them to be compassionate towards others, including people from different backgrounds or those facing challenges. Engage in acts of kindness together, such as volunteering or helping those in need.

Encourage critical thinking: Foster critical thinking skills in your child by encouraging them to question and evaluate situations from an ethical standpoint. Teach them to analyze the potential consequences of their actions and how they may impact others. Encourage them to make thoughtful decisions based on moral principles.

Use stories and examples: Stories, fables, and parables can be powerful tools for teaching moral values. Share stories that highlight virtues like honesty, courage, and integrity. Discuss the lessons learned from these stories and connect them to real-life situations your child may encounter.

Encourage moral reasoning: As your child grows older, encourage them to think through moral dilemmas and make ethical choices independently. Ask them questions that stimulate moral reasoning, such as "What would you do in this situation?" or "Why do you think this action is right or wrong?"

Promote cultural and religious values: If you have specific cultural or religious values, share them with your child and explain their significance. This can provide a moral framework and help shape their understanding of right and wrong.

Reinforce positive peer influences: Encourage your child to spend time with peers who share similar values. Positive peer influences can reinforce moral values and provide opportunities for your child to practice and strengthen their ethical behavior.

Be patient and consistent: Instilling moral values is an ongoing process that requires patience and consistency. Children may make mistakes or exhibit behaviors contrary to the values you're trying to teach. In such situations, provide guidance, reinforce positive behavior, and offer opportunities for growth and learning.

Remember that each child is unique, and the pace at which they develop moral values may vary. By providing guidance, being a positive role model, and fostering open communication, you can help instill strong moral values in your child and prepare them for a responsible and ethical adulthood.

Teaching Responsibility and Empathy
Teaching responsibility and empathy are important aspects of a well-rounded education and upbringing. These qualities help individuals become more considerate, compassionate, and accountable for their actions. Here are some strategies and principles you can apply to promote responsibility and empathy in teaching:

Lead by example: Children and students learn a great deal from observing the behavior of adults and authority figures. Model responsible and empathetic behavior in your own actions, interactions, and decision-making processes. Be aware of how your words and actions impact others and strive to demonstrate the qualities you wish to cultivate in your students.

Foster a supportive and inclusive classroom environment: Create a safe and welcoming space where students feel comfortable expressing themselves and sharing their thoughts and emotions. Encourage open dialogue, active listening, and respect for diverse perspectives. By promoting inclusivity, students can develop empathy by recognizing and appreciating the experiences and feelings of others.

Incorporate literature and media: Use literature, films, and other media as tools to explore different perspectives and encourage empathy. Choose stories and characters that deal with social issues, moral dilemmas, and complex emotions. Discuss these narratives, encouraging students to put themselves in the shoes of the characters, analyze their motivations, and consider the consequences of their actions.

Engage in service learning and community projects: Encourage students to actively participate in service-learning initiatives and community projects. These activities provide practical opportunities to develop empathy by engaging with people from different backgrounds and circumstances. Whether it's volunteering at a local shelter, organizing a charity event, or participating in community cleanup efforts, these experiences foster a sense of responsibility and empathy towards others.

Practice perspective-taking exercises: Engage students in activities that require them to imagine the world from another person's point of view. This could involve role-playing scenarios, writing exercises, or discussions where students take on the perspective of different individuals or groups. By encouraging students to consider the thoughts, feelings, and needs of others, they can develop empathy and a deeper understanding of diverse experiences.

Encourage responsibility through autonomy and accountability: Provide students with opportunities to make decisions and take responsibility for their actions. Foster autonomy by involving them in classroom management, project planning, and problem-solving. Encourage reflection on their choices and actions, discussing the consequences and how they can learn from both successes and mistakes.

Promote conflict resolution skills: Teach students effective communication, negotiation, and conflict resolution strategies. Help them understand the importance of listening to others, finding common ground, and seeking mutually beneficial solutions. By equipping students with these skills, you empower them to handle conflicts and disagreements in responsible and empathetic ways.

Teaching responsibility and empathy is an ongoing process that requires consistency, patience, and reinforcement. By incorporating these strategies into your teaching approach, you can help students develop a strong sense of responsibility and empathy, which will benefit them throughout their lives.

Promoting Social Consciousness and Philanthropy
Promoting social consciousness and philanthropy is essential for creating a positive impact on society and addressing various social issues. Here are some ways you can promote social consciousness and philanthropy:

Educate and raise awareness: Start by educating yourself about social issues and philanthropic causes. Stay updated on current events and understand the root causes and impact of these issues. Share your knowledge with others through conversations, social media, or even organizing awareness campaigns or workshops.

Lead by example: Practice what you preach by incorporating social consciousness and philanthropy into your own life. Volunteer your time, donate to causes you care about, and engage in acts of kindness and compassion. When others see your actions, they may be inspired to follow suit.

Engage in meaningful conversations: Initiate conversations about social issues and philanthropy with friends, family, colleagues, or within your community. Encourage open dialogue, listen to different perspectives, and promote empathy and understanding. These conversations can raise awareness, challenge assumptions, and inspire collective action.

Support local nonprofits and community organizations: Research and identify local nonprofits and community organizations that align with your values and support causes you care about. Donate your resources, whether it's money, time, or skills, to assist their efforts. You can also consider organizing fundraisers or volunteer events to support these organizations.

Utilize social media platforms: Leverage the power of social media to amplify social consciousness and philanthropic messages. Share stories and information about various causes, advocate for positive change, and encourage others to get involved. Utilize hashtags, join online campaigns, and connect with like-minded individuals and organizations.

Practice conscious consumerism: Make ethical and socially responsible choices in your purchasing habits. Support businesses that prioritize sustainability, fair trade practices, and social impact. By supporting such businesses, you encourage others to adopt similar practices and contribute to positive change.

Collaborate and network: Join forces with others who share your passion for social consciousness and philanthropy. Collaborate with local organizations, community leaders, or even start your own initiatives. By working together, you can combine resources, skills, and ideas to create a more significant impact.

Advocate for policy changes: Recognize that many social issues require systemic changes. Engage in advocacy efforts by contacting elected officials, signing petitions, and participating in peaceful protests or demonstrations. Use your voice to influence policy decisions and support legislation that promotes social justice and equality.

promoting social consciousness and philanthropy is an ongoing process. Small, consistent actions can lead to meaningful change over time. By inspiring others and fostering a culture of empathy and giving, we can work towards creating a better and more equitable world for everyone.